Acknowledgements

Pitkin Publishing would like to thank Ray Anderson who kindly gave permission to reproduce his collection of Home Front material

Developed and produced by Ivor Claydon Graphics
Edited by David Notley
Cover design by Tokiko Morishima

First published in this form © Pitkin Publishing 1998
Latest reprint 2019

Available through mail order
See our website (www.pavilionbooks.com) for our full range of titles or contact us for a copy of our brochure:
Pitkin Publishing, Pavilion Books Company Limited,
43 Great Ormond St, London WC1N 3HZ
Sales and enquiries: 020 7462 1500
Email: sales@pavilionbooks.com

Printed and bound in Slovenia   15/19
ISBN 978-1-84165-264-1

WARTIME RECIPES

A COLLECTION OF RECIPES FROM THE WAR YEARS

DIG FOR VICTORY

PITKIN

Contents

Victorian Scotch Broth

4 carrots
3 turnips
3 onions
2.2 litres/4 pints of water or vegetable stock
75g/3oz pearl barley
1 teaspoonful of chopped parsley
Salt and pepper

Wash, peel and dice the vegetables, put the water or stock into a saucepan and bring to the boil, add the vegetables. Wash the barley and add, let all simmer till the vegetables are soft and barley cooked. Season, sprinkle the parsley in the bottom of a tureen, pour the boiling soup on to it and serve.

Cooking Time: 1 1/2 hours/8 Helpings

Haricot Soup

450g/1lb haricot beans
1 onion
2 small potatoes
1.1 litres/2 pints of vegetable stock or water
150ml/1/4 pint milk (if liked)
Seasoning

Wash the beans and soak overnight in cold water. Put into a pan with the stock and the water they were soaked in. Let it come to the boil. Skim. Wash, peel and slice the vegetables and add. Simmer all gently for two hours or till the beans are tender. Rub all through a sieve. Add the milk. Return to the pan and boil. Season and serve.

Cooking Time: 3 hours/6 Helpings

Potato Soup

450g/1lb of peeled potatoes
1 onion
A little fat
900ml/1 1/2 pints of water
Pepper and salt
300ml/1/2 pint milk

Cut up the potatoes, slice the onion and just
brown it in a little fat. Add the potatoes and
water, pepper and salt to taste, bring to the boil
and simmer for two hours. Pass through a sieve,
add 300ml/1/2 pint of milk and make very hot.
Cooking Time: 3 hours/6 Helpings

Barley Soup

50g/2oz of pearl barley
450g/1lb carrots and turnips
A sprig of parsley
A small piece of celery
2 good-sized onions
Salt and pepper
Sufficient water to make in all 2.2 litres/4 pints
300ml/1/2 pint of milk

Cover the barley with water and soak overnight.
Put it into a casserole with the carrots and
turnips sliced, adding the parsley, celery, onions,
salt, pepper and water. Bring it to the boil and
simmer very gently until the barley is done. Rub
it through a wire sieve, add 300ml/1/2 pint of milk,
bring it to the boil again and serve.
Cooking Time: 2 hours/8 Helpings

FOOD FACTS

**A LITTLE
EXTRA WILL
MAKE A
DIFFERENCE**

Try serving some of
the following with
your favourite soup.

DUMPLINGS
Mix 8oz flour with
1 teaspoonful of
baking powder and
1 teaspoonful of
dried herbs. Form
into a firm dough
with cold water.
Drop into soup and
cook quickly for 10
minutes.

CROUTONS
Take a few slices of
wheatmeal bread,
dice and bake in a
hot oven until crisp.

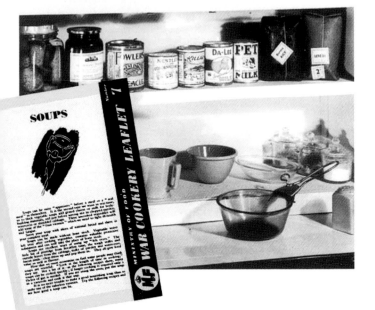

MINISTRY OF FOOD
WAR COOKERY LEAFLET 7

Spinach Soup with Dumplings

450g/1lb spinach
1 turnip
2 onions
1 small head of celery
2 carrots
A little thyme and parsley
600ml/1 pint of stock
12g/½ oz of clarified fat
Pepper and salt
1.1 litres/2 pints of water

Cut up the vegetables and stew all together till tender, pass through a sieve. Add to the veg-etable pulp and liquor 1.1litres/2 pints of water, and boil together. Have ready 2 small dumplings for each person, put them in the tureen and pour the boiling soup on to them and serve.
Cooking Time: 2 hours/4 Helpings

Dumplings

225g/½lb flour
25g/1oz of dripping or any fat
Water and salt

Rub the dripping into the flour, add salt. Moisten with a little water, form into balls the size of a marble and drop into boiling water or stock; cook about for 30 minutes.
Cooking Time: 30 minutes/8 Helpings

Parsnip Soup

4 parsnips
1 onion
1.7 litres/3 pints of good stock
Some well-scaled bacon rinds, if available
25g/1oz of fat
25g/1oz of rice
Salt and pepper
A pinch of ground mace

Chop the onion finely and fry in the fat, then add the parsnips, which should have been washed and grated, then the rice, stock and bacon rinds. Bring to the boil, season and simmer gently for 1½ hours. Test, season again if required, remove the bacon rinds, put through a sieve and serve very hot. Turnip soup may be made in the same way, and if a little milk can be allowed it improves the soup. Too much soft food is not good for the digestion, therefore some cubes of fried bread or toast crusts well browned in the oven should be served with the soup.

Cooking Time: 2 hours/6 Helpings

Gravy Soup

900g/2lb shin of beef
450g/1lb onions or leeks
1/2 tin tomatoes
450g/1lb carrots or 1 tin (use liquid as stock)
100g/1/4lb fat
75g/3oz flour
2.2 litres/4 pints stock or water
Salt and pepper

The Ministry of
Food wants your
cooking secrets

Shred or chop vegetables and fry in the fat until a
golden brown. Add flour and brown. Add meat,
cut into small pieces; add liquid slowly. Season
and cook slowly for 3 to 4 hours, adding tomatoes 30 minutes before serving, and a little
colouring if necessary. Strain through a sieve or
colander and re-heat.
Cooking Time: 4 hours/10 Helpings

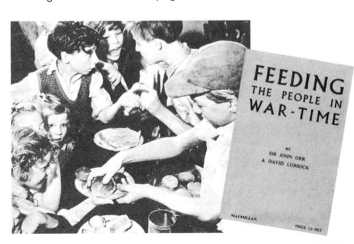

FEEDING
THE PEOPLE IN
WAR-TIME

BY
SIR JOHN ORR
& DAVID LUBBOCK

MACMILLAN   PRICE 1/- NET

FOOD FACTS

There are some recipes here for cooking such things as liver, tripe, kidneys and so on. There are some suggestions for cooking the cheaper cuts of meat.

Beef Hash

450g/1lb cold salt beef
450g/1lb cold cooked potatoes
Milk
Salt and pepper
1 onion, finely chopped
25g/1oz margarine

Mince the salt beef and mix it with the cold potatoes, which should be crumbled but not mashed, and finely chopped onion. Season with salt and pepper, add enough milk to moisten, and stir until all are well mixed together. Make the margarine hot in a large frying pan. Spread the mixture all over the pan and put over a low gas, where it can cook slowly. Cook gently for 40-45 minutes. Loosen with a knife and turn on to a hot dish, folding the mixture in two.
Cooking Time: 1 hour/6-8 Helpings

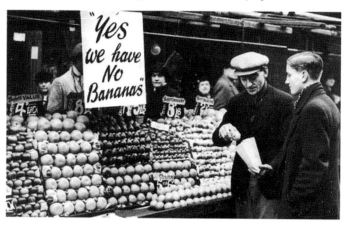

Devilled Fish

225g/8oz cold cooked fish
1 hard-boiled egg, sliced or chopped
37g/1½ oz stale breadcrumbs
Pinch of cayenne
Pinch of grated nutmeg
Pinch of curry powder
½ teaspoonful made mustard
2 teaspoonfuls Worcester sauce or
    tomato ketchup
25g/1oz margarine
25g/1oz flour
300ml/½ pint of milk
Salt and pepper

Flake the fish and remove skin and bones. Brush a pie-dish with melted margarine. Melt 25g/1oz of margarine in a saucepan, stir in the flour and cook till it bubbles. Take off the heat and add 300ml/½ pint of milk and water. Bring to the boil, lower the heat and cook for 3 minutes, stirring all the time. Add the fish, egg, nutmeg, curry powder, cayenne, mustard and Worcester sauce or ketchup. Taste, and season with salt and pepper. Pour into prepared dish, coat with breadcrumbs, and bake for 20 minutes in a moderately hot oven.
Cooking Time: 2 hours/ 4-6 Helpings

FOOD FACTS

Trade considerations and many of our food likes and dislikes will have to go by the board. With sufficient milk, vegetables and potatoes, there need be no malnutrition. With sufficient bread, fat (butter or margarine), potatoes and oatmeal, there will be no starvation.

'Don't want to go to bed – till I've had my OXO.'

How Bobbie loves his nightly cup of OXO. Children of all ages like its rich beefy flavour . . . wise mothers know that OXO's good for the whole family.

My! OXO!

Roast Hearts

2 sheep's hearts
I tablespoonful breadcrumbs
I teaspoonful shredded suet
Salt and pepper
A little milk
Dripping
I level tablespoonful self-raising flour
Parsley

Mix the breadcrumbs, seasoning, parsley and salt, and bind with a little milk. Wash the hearts thoroughly, cut away the pipes from the top and cut the dividing walls. Stuff the hearts, fold the flaps over and keep in place with a skewer.
Heat sufficient dripping in a strong saucepan to come 12mm/¹/₂ inch up the sides. Put in the hearts and brown them all over, reduce the heat and cook gently for I hour, turning from time to time. Lift out the hearts, strain off most of the fat and make the gravy by sprinkling a level tablespoonful of self-raising flour into the fat. Stir until brown, season and add vegetable water or hot water. Stir and bring to the boil.
Cooking Time: 2 hours/2 Helpings

The combined effect of propaganda and fall in price is well seen in the case of fruit. In 1900, the price of a banana was 2d. By 1937, it had fallen to 1d. The consumption of bananas between these dates increased from 2¹/₂ million to 20 million bunches. In 1920-3, the average price of grapefruit was 6d. By 1935, it had fallen to 3d. The annual consumption increased from 1,200 tons to 59,500 tons. The fall in price was accompanied by the 'eat more fruit' campaign.

Tripe and Onions

450g/1lb tripe
2 large onions
Salt and pepper
600ml/1 pint milk and water
25g/1oz self-raising flour

Bring the onions to the boil, then slice thinly.
Wash the tripe thoroughly and cut into pieces.
Put the tripe and onions in a saucepan, season
and cover with the milk and water. Simmer for 2
hours. Mix the flour to a smooth paste with a little milk, then stir this paste into the tripe and
onions. Stir and boil for 5 minutes and serve.
Cooking Time: 3 hours/6 Helpings

Corned Beef Rissoles

100g/4oz corned beef
225g/8oz mashed potatoes
225g/8oz cooked mixed vegetables
100g/4oz wheatmeal breadcrumbs
seasoning
pinch mixed herbs
4 tablespoons brown sauce or
vegetable water

Crumb the corned beef and mix with
the mashed cooked vegetables and
breadcrumbs. Season and add the
mixed herbs. Bind the mixture with
brown sauce or vegetable water, form
into round shapes. Bake in a hot
oven.
Cooking Time: 20 minutes/2-3 Helpings

Fillets of Pork

225g/8oz pork sausagemeat
225g/8oz potatoes
Pinch of sage
100g/4oz breadcrumbs
150ml/¼ pint vegetable stock
1 tablespoon of flour
Pepper and salt

RECIPE of the WEEK

Leek Sauce
½ pint milk and water
half a leek, chopped
Salt and pepper
1oz flour
Pinch of herbs

Put some of the milk, or milk and water, leek and seasoning into a pan and allow to simmer slowly for 15 to 20 minutes. Blend the flour with the remaining cold milk, stir into the pan with the leek, etc., and cook for 1-2 minutes.

Flake the pork sausagemeat (with the outside fat removed), then mix in the mashed potatoes and crisp breadcrumbs. Season well with pepper and salt, adding a pinch of sage if liked. Then bind with a thick sauce made from the meat juices taken from the tin, and made up to 1 teacup measure with vegetable stock and flour plus a little of the pork fat from the tin. Divide into nine or ten sections, shape into finger rolls, coat in more crumbs, and fry or bake until heated through and crisp-coated, with a light greasing of pork fat for the frying pan or baking tin.

These are delicious by themselves, or served with Leek Sauce.
Cooking Time: 2 hours/6 Helpings

ME FOR
McDougall's
SELF-RAISING FLOUR

Mince Slices

225g/8oz mince (any cooked meat)
100g/4oz cooked mashed potatoes
100g/4oz stale breadcrumbs
Salt and pepper

Mix well together the mince, mashed potatoes, breadcrumbs and salt and pepper. Turn out onto a floured board and roll into an oblong, ¼ inch thick. Cut into slices and fry in a small quantity of hot fat, or grill for 5-7 minutes. Serve with mashed potatoes and a green vegetable.
Cooking Time: 1 hour/4-6 Helpings

Savoury Meat Roll

350g/12oz sausage meat
100g/4oz stale bread
125g/5oz pinto beans, cooked and mashed
Pepper and salt
1 teaspoon made mustard
1 teaspoon thyme
Gravy browning
Breadcrumbs

Soak the stale bread in water until soft. Squeeze out the water and mash the bread with the sausage meat, the mashed beans, pepper, salt, made mustard and thyme. Add gravy browning until the mixture is a rich brown. Press very firmly into a greased 2lb stone jam jar or tin and steam for 2 hours. Roll in browned breadcrumbs and serve hot with brown gravy, or cold with a raw cabbage heart salad and boiled potatoes.
Cooking Time: 3 hours/6 Helpings

American Mince

150g/6oz corned beef, minced or finely chopped
225g/8oz cooked pearl barley
$^1/_2$ pint tomato pulp
salt and pepper
25g/1oz cheese, grated
25g/1oz breadcrumbs
12g/$^1/_2$ oz dripping or margarine
2 tomatoes (if available)

Place the beef, barley, tomato pulp, seasoning, cheese and breadcrumbs in layers in a greased pie dish. Finish with a layer of cheese and dot with the dripping or margarine. Bake in a moderate oven for 25 minutes. Slice the whole tomatoes and spread over the top. Return to the oven for a further 15 minutes.
Cooking Time: 1 hour/4-6 Helpings

Liver and Bacon with Rice

450g/1lb liver
225g/8oz rice
225g/8oz bacon
150ml/¼ pint of good stock
150ml/1 tablespoonful of flour

Fry the bacon and then remove and keep hot.
Then fry the sliced liver in the bacon fat until
brown. Remove and keep hot. Add and stir the
flour to the pan juices, before adding the stock,
salt and pepper. Stir until the sauce begins to boil.
Have ready a good dish of boiled rice, arrange
the liver and bacon on it and pour the sauce
over the top.
Cooking Time: 1 hour/6 Helpings

Smothered Sausages

225g/8oz sausages
1lb mashed potatoes
Salt and pepper
150ml/¼ pint of hot milk
1 tablespoonful chopped parsley
1oz margarine

Put the sausages in a saucepan of cold water and
bring to the boil. Remove the skins and put each
sausage in flour. Brush a fireproof dish with melted margarine, lay the sausages in and sprinkle
with salt and pepper. Boil the potatoes and mash
adding a knob of margarine, the hot milk and
beat well. Season well and spread over the
sausages. Brush with a little milk and decorate
with a fork. Bake for 30 minutes in a hot oven.
Cooking Time: 1 hour/4 Helpings

Beef à la Mode

675g/1 ½lb stewing steak
2 large onions
3 carrots
2 bay leaves
50g/2oz margarine
2 tablespoonfuls of vinegar
Salt and pepper
2 cloves

Lay the pieces of beef in a deep dish. Cut the onions and carrots in slices and lay them with the cloves and bay leaves on top of the meat. Pour the vinegar over the meat and leave it to soak overnight. Heat the margarine in a casserole, put in the meat and cook first on one side, then on the other. Put in the onions, carrots, bay leaves, salt and pepper to taste and add enough cold water to just cover the meat. Cook on a gentle heat for 5 hours. This long cooking is necessary either on a ring or oven for the success of the dish.
Cooking Time: 6 hours/6-8 Helpings

Savoury Tripe Casserole

225g/8oz tripe
I sheep's kidney
100g/4oz calf's liver
25g/Ioz margarine
I carrot, cut into slices
I onion, sliced
I bay leaf
I tablespoonful flour
Salt and pepper
$^1/_2$ teaspoonful mixed herbs

Cut the tripe into strips and the liver into slices. Wash the kidney, remove the fat and cut into small pieces. Mix the flour, season generously with salt and pepper together with the herbs. Toss the tripe, liver and kidneys in the seasoned flour. Melt the margarine in a casserole dish and make it hot. Put in the meat, the carrot and onion and fry together for a few minutes. Pour in enough boiling water just to cover the ingredients, add the bay leaf and simmer gently over a low heat, or in a moderate oven for 2 hours. Serve hot in the casserole with dumplings if you wish.
Cooking Time: 3 hours/6 Helpings

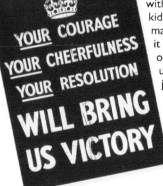

YOUR **COURAGE**
YOUR **CHEERFULNESS**
YOUR **RESOLUTION**
WILL BRING
US VICTORY

GREEN VEGETABLES

No country in the world grows better vegetables than we do, and probably no country in the world treats them worse. For generations we have ruined our vegetables by careless peeling and our haste in cooking, and baled most of the goodness out of green vegetables—literally poured it down the sink. In proof that such methods are favourably enough, to wartime they are well worthwhile.

There is no need to worry about the running down of important foods in wartime if we eat home-grown vegetables, especially if we learn to eat them raw as well as cooked. This insofar as health do, for the extra eye as well as cooked. This insofar as health do, for the extra eye as well cannot, but within for the first time, the variety of salads flavours that salad provide.

True, two classes of people will suffer if we make full use of our vegetable crops. First, the cookers of potato orders and whose tastes will be less to demand. Secondly the outdoor our too-happy unstudied sauces demand. Secondly the outdoor our too-happy unstudied sauces demand, flavour of to good feelings, will no palates ever waiter occasion well-cooking vegetables, content with the delicious flavour of

Once we have discovered that vegetables can be a delight, we shall come to think of them merely as something to serve with meat. We shall eat them for honour of wings to rates them wives, we shall help them upon their own, cooked, and rightly, as one of our most important sources of health and strength.

MINISTRY OF FOOD
WAR COOKERY LEAFLET
Number 10

Savoury Onions

RECIPE of the WEEK

4 medium onions
50g/2oz cheese, grated
Salt and pepper
I egg or I reconstituted egg
$^1/_2$ teacupful soft breadcrumbs
12g/$^1/_2$oz melted margarine
I teaspoonful chopped sage

Peel the onions, put into boiling salted water and cook steadily for 30 minutes. Lift the onions out of the liquid, save $^1/_2$ teacup of this. Remove the centres of the onions, chop this finely and blend with the breadcrumbs, sage, cheese and egg. Season the mixture and fill the onion cases then put these into a casserole with $^1/_2$ teacup of onion stock. Brush the onions with the melted margarine. Cover the casserole and bake for 45 minutes in the centre of a moderately hot oven.
Cooking Time: 2 hours/4 Helpings

Turnip Top Salad

100g/4oz turnip tops
100g/4oz white cabbage heart
50g/2oz raw beetroot
50g/2oz raw carrots
Salad dressing
Watercress for garnishing

Grate or shred all the vegetables separately and arrange attractively on a large dish. Sprinkle with salad dressing and decorate with watercress. Make the salad dressing by adding vinegar, a little mustard, pepper and salt to a white sauce.
Cooking Time: 20 minutes/6 Helpings

SALAD SUGGESTIONS

Well-shredded spinach, heart of cabbage, leaves of spring greens, make a delicious salad base. And you've no idea until you try them how tasty young dandelion leaves can be.
Choose young leaves, wash, chop finely and mix with any raw shredded root vegetables. A little sugar is a help in this kind of salad.

FOOD
IS AMMUNITION OF WAR
DON'T WASTE IT

Pathfinder Pudding

It is worthwhile considering alternatives to meat dishes these days. Recipes containing different forms of body-building material, such as cheese, beans and lentils can be served either as an extra dish, or as the main dish of the meal.

SUET PASTRY
150g/6oz national flour
$^1/_2$ teaspoonful salt
$^3/_4$ teaspoonful baking powder
25g/1 oz suet, chopped or grated
40g/1 $^1/_2$ oz uncooked potato, shredded
Water
FILLING
900g/2lb cooked parsnips, diced
100g/4oz cheese, grated
1 uncooked leek, sliced
$^1/_2$ teaspoon mustard powder
Pepper
1 teaspoon salt

Mix the flour, salt and baking powder, add the suet, potato and water to bind. Roll out three-quarters of the pastry to line a 1.1 litre/2 pint greased basin. Mix the parsnips, cheese, leek, mustard, pepper and salt together. Put into the lined basin. Roll out the remaining quarter of pastry to form a lid. Put this into the pudding, cover with an up-turned saucer and steam for 2 hours.

Cooking Time: 3 hours/6-8 Helpings

Vegetable Casserole

450g/1lb each of potatoes, onions and carrots
450g/1lb cooked haricot beans
450g/1lb tomatoes
1 large cauliflower
225g/½lb cooked macaroni or spaghetti
2.2 litres/4 pints of water
100g/4oz margarine

Wash and peel the potatoes and carrots and cut
them into smallish pieces. Peel and slice the
onions. Wash the cauliflower, pull off all the flo-
rets and slice the stalk and the green leaves. Put
into a casserole with the margarine, add salt and
water. Bring to the boil and simmer gently for 40
minutes. After 20 minutes, add the tomatoes and
the cooked haricots. Cook the macaroni separately in boiling salted water and put into the
stew, season and serve.
Cooking Time 2 hours/12 Helpings

DOs AND DON'Ts WITH VEGETABLES

DO serve swedes when greens are short, or for a change. Of all the root vegetables, swedes are rich in Vitamin C.

DO provide at least one pound of pota-toes per head every day and less bread.

DO cook potatoes in their skins, this prevents their goodness dissolving into the water.

DO serve some-thing green and raw every day.

DON'T soak veg-etables long, their vitamins and miner-als seep out into the water.

DON'T throw veg-etable water away, use it for soups and sauces.

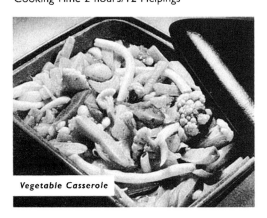

Vegetable Casserole

Tomato Macaroni au Gratin

VEGETABLE MIXTURES

Here are some good vegetable mixtures which will be popular now that we may have to eat more vegetables than we did:

1 Baked or steamed potatoes, baked or boiled onions and brussels sprouts.

2 Cauliflower and carrots, cooked separately, but served together.

3 Potatoes baked in their jackets, and carrots or parsnips par-boiled and baked in the oven with a little margarine until they are brown.

4 Carrots, swedes and turnips, all mashed together with hot milk.

225g/8oz macaroni
$\frac{1}{2}$ tin tomatoes
100g/4 oz cheese
1 small onion, chopped
50g/2oz margarine
3 springs of parsley
Salt and pepper
1 tablespoonful stale breadcrumbs

Brush a deep pie dish with melted margarine. Cook the macaroni in boiling water for 20 minutes, then test a piece between the teeth. If it is soft, drain off the water (which should be kept to make sauce or soup). While the macaroni is cooking, melt the margarine in a saucepan, cook the chopped onion in it until soft, draw the pan off the heat, add the tomatoes, parsley, salt and pepper and leave the mixture to simmer for 30 minutes. Then put the macaroni into the saucepan with the sauce, season with salt and pepper, add the grated cheese and stir well. Turn into the prepared dish and scatter the breadcrumbs over the top. Put into a quick oven for 15 minutes at 210°C (425°F or Mark 7) and serve hot.
Cooking Time: 2 hours/6-8 Helpings

The Ministry of Food wants your cooking secrets

PIG
FOOD

WASTE FOOD
FOR THE FEEDING OF PIGS

Put IN Bin.
Potato and Apple Peelings
Pea Shells
Scraps of Meat
Waste Bread
Cabbage, Lettuce Leaves
etc, etc.

Do NOT put in Bin.
Rhubarb or Potato Tops
Tea Leaves
Coffee Grounds
Skins of Oranges, Lemons,
Grape Fruit or Bananas
Salt, Soap or Soda

PLEASE KEEP AS DRY AS POSSIBLE
AND REPLACE LID OF BIN

Mock Duck

450g/1lb red lentils
2 large onions
$\frac{1}{2}$ teaspoonful of sage
$\frac{1}{2}$ teaspoonful sweet herbs
100g/4oz rice or mashed potatoes
25g/1oz fat
Brown sauce

Wash the lentils, mince and fry the onions lightly, add the lentils, and 2.2 litres/4 pints of stock, bring to the boil and simmer until the lentils are soft. Add the potatoes or rice, sage and herbs, and season well. Shape as much like a duck as possible and place on a greased baking sheet and bake in a hot oven till brown. Baste often. Serve on a hot dish with brown sauce poured round. The lentils will absorb the stock; if they get too dry before they are soft, add more stock. If rice is used instead of potatoes, cook it with lentils.
Cooking Time 2 hours/4-6 Helpings

Potatoes au Gratin

900g/2lb cold cooked potatoes
300ml/¹⁄2 pint milk
100g/4oz grated cheese
50g/2oz margarine
2 tablespoonfuls stale breadcrumbs
Salt and pepper

Mash the potatoes thoroughly in a saucepan with
300ml/¹⁄2 pint of boiling milk and 38g/1¹⁄2ozs margarine. Take the pan from the heat, season with
salt and pepper and add the grated cheese. Brush
a pie-dish with melted margarine, put the potato
mixture into it, smooth it neatly and brush with
the remaining margarine, melted. Scatter the stale
breadcrumbs over the top and put into a hot
oven for 15 minutes.
Cooking Time: 40 minutes/6-8 Helpings

Those who have
"dug for victory"
will surely be inter-
ested in new ways
of cooking and
serving young car-
rots, their early
peas and new pota-
toes, not to speak
of the wealth of
green stuff that will
be coming along in
late spring and
summer.

Your own vegetables
all the year round...

if you

DIG FOR
VICTORY NOW

Caramel and Semolina Mould

50g/2oz sugar
4 tablespoonfuls water
600ml/1 pint milk or milk and water
1 tablespoonful apricot jam or marmalade
75g/3oz semolina

Put the sugar and 2 tablespoons of water into a
saucepan, stir until the sugar has dissolved, then
boil until a golden caramel. Add the remaining
water and heat until blended, cool slightly then
pour into a basin or mould. Meanwhile bring the
milk or milk and water to the boil in a separate
pan, add the jam or marmalade, whisk in the
semolina and cook steadily for 10-15 minutes,
stirring most of the time. Allow to cool and stiff-
en slightly, stir briskly then spoon over the
caramel and allow to set. Turn out to serve.
Cooking Time: 1 hour/6 Helpings

Eggless Sponge Pudding

150g/6oz self-raising flour or plain flour
1 1/2 teaspoonfuls baking powder
50g/2oz margarine or cooking fat
50g/2oz sugar
1 tablespoonful golden syrup
1/4 teaspoonful bicarbonate of soda
1 dessertspoonful vinegar
Milk to mix

Sift the flour or flour and baking powder, rub in the margarine or cooking fat, add the sugar and golden syrup. Blend the bicarbonate of soda with the vinegar, add to the other ingredients, with enough milk to make a sticky consistency. Put the mixture into a greased basin, allowing room to rise. Cover with a plate or margarine paper. Steam for 1 1/4-1 1/2 hours or until firm. Serve hot with fruit or jam.

VARIATIONS
A little golden syrup or jam could be put into the basin before adding the sponge mixture.
Cooking Time: 2 hours/4-6 Helpings

FOOD FACTS

EVERY CRUMB COUNTS
Never throw away stale bread. Use it as breadcrumbs in savoury and sweet puddings, in a breakfast cereal, or crushed for coatings. Soak, squeeze and beat up with a fork for sweet and savoury puddings, etc.

Bread Pudding

A Bread Pudding is an excellent way to use up bread. The recipe below can be varied in many ways, for example if you are short of dried fruit use a diced cooking apple or a little more marmalade. Slices of Bread Pudding are ideal to tuck into a packed meal box for a factory worker.

225g/8oz stale bread
50g/2oz grated suet
25g/1oz sugar
1 tablespoonful marmalade
50g/2oz dried fruit
1 reconsituted dried egg
Milk to mix
Ground cinnamon

Put the bread into a basin, add cold water and leave for 15 minutes then squeeze dry with your fingers. Return the bread to the basin, add all the other ingredients, with enough milk to make a sticky consistency. If the spice is added last you can make quite certain you have the right amount. Put into a greased Yorkshire pudding tin and bake in the centre of a slow oven for 1 1/2 hours or steam in a greased basin for 2 hours. Remove from the steamer or oven and allow to cool for 10 minutes. Serve on its own or with custard or condensed milk.
Cooking Time: 3 hours/6 Helpings

Steamed Date Pudding

75g/3oz self-raising flour
50g/2oz stale breadcrumbs
50g/2oz margarine
225g/8oz dates, stoned and chopped
1 tablespoonful golden syrup
$^1/_2$ teaspoonful cinnamon and nutmeg
Pinch of salt
150ml/$^1/_4$ pint of milk

Brush a pudding basin with melted margarine.
Add to the rest of the melted margarine the
golden syrup and the milk, heated together. Mix
together the flour, breadcrumbs, spices, salt and
chopped dates. Pour the milk etc., on to the mixture and stir well until it is moist all through. Put
into the prepared basin, cover with doubled
paper brushed with melted margarine and steam
for 2$^1/_2$ hours. Serve with lemon sauce.
Cooking Time: 3 hours/4-6 Helpings

Prune Pudding

450g/1lb prunes, soaked in 300ml/$\frac{1}{2}$ pint cold water
2 tablespoonfuls golden syrup
Piece of stick cinnamon
450ml/$\frac{3}{4}$ pint boiling water
2 tablespoonfuls lemon juice
100g/4oz cornflour

Soak the prunes overnight. Simmer them in the water they were soaked in with 2 tablespoonfuls of golden syrup. Remove the stones and simmer in the syrup, with the cinnamon and boiling water, for 10 minutes. Blend the cornflour with a little cold water and add to the prune mixture. Boil for 5 minutes stirring all the time. Add the lemon juice, remove the cinnamon and pour into a wetted mould. Leave to set in a mould and serve with thick cream or custard sauce.
Cooking Time: 30 minutes/4-6 Helpings

Prune Pudding

Date and Raisin Pudding

150g/6oz self-raising flour
50g/2oz margarine
50g/2oz dates, stoned and cut into pieces
50g/2oz raisins, stoned
Pinch of bicarbonate of soda
1 teaspoonful golden syrup
Milk to mix
Pinch of salt

Brush a pudding basin and a doubled paper with melted margarine. Sift the flour, carbonate of soda and salt and rub in the margarine. Add the dates and raisins. Mix to a fairly soft consistency with the milk and golden syrup. Put into the prepared basin, cover with prepared paper and steam for 1 1/2 hours. Serve with custard sauce.
Cooking Time: 2 hours/4-6 Helpings

Spotted Dick

Members are requested to rinse and
RETURN PROMPTLY
empty Colco
MILK BOTTLES
Bottle shortage is now acute, new
stocks being difficult to obtain

The Committee have decided that
in future all Dividend accruing on
SHARE NO. 10,000
shall be equally divided between the
Aid for Russia Fund and the Aid for
China Fund

COLCHESTER CO-OPERATIVE SOCIETY, LIMITED

225g/8oz self-raising flour
75g/3oz shredded suet
1/2 teaspoonful salt
50g/2oz sugar
75g/3oz currants
50g/2oz sultanas
Water or milk to mix

Sift the flour and salt into a basin, add the suet, sugar and fruit and mix to a moderately soft dough, with the milk. Put into a greased basin, cover the top with a greased paper and steam for 2 1/2 hours. When cooked turn out and serve with custard.
Cooking Time: 3 hours/6-8 Helpings

Apple Cocada

6 cooking apples
100g/4oz desiccated coconut
300ml/½ pint milk
2-4 tablespoonfuls soft brown sugar
25g/1oz margarine

Soak the coconut in milk for an hour. Brush a pie-dish with melted margarine, put a layer of coconut. Peel, core and quarter the apples, put a layer of these into the dish. Sprinkle with sugar and dot with margarine. Repeat these layers once, adding enough sugar to sweeten the apples. Bake for an hour in a moderate oven.
Cooking Time: 2 hours/4-6 Helpings

Honey Walnut Pudding

100g/4oz self-raising flour
50g/2oz stale breadcrumbs
1 egg, beaten
4 tablespoonsful honey
50g/2oz shelled walnuts
50g/2oz margarine
2 teaspoonfuls vanilla essence
1 teacupful milk

Brush a pie dish with melted margarine. With the rest of the melted margarine mix the milk, honey and the beaten egg and warm gently. Mix the flour, breadcrumbs and walnuts, roughly chopped, in a basin. Add the vanilla to the milk mixture and pour it on to the flour, etc. Mix, pour into the pie dish and bake for 1 hour in a warm oven 180°C (350°F or Mark 4). Serve with honey.
Cooking Time: 2 hours/4-6 Helpings

Brown Betty

225g/8oz stale breadcrumbs
900g/2lb apples
2 tablespoonfuls golden syrup
1/4 teaspoonful grated nutmeg
1 teaspoonful cinnamon
50g/2oz margarine
1 teacupful of water
1 lemon

There is thus no need for the public to worry about the food position so far as supplies are concerned. The difficulty in war is the same as it was in peacetime, not one of supply but one of more equal distribution of the food which is available.

Brush a pie dish with melted margarine. Put a layer of stale breadcrumbs at the bottom. Cover with a layer of grated apples. It is not necessary to peel the apples; they are better grated whole. Put half the golden syrup over the apples. Dot with margarine and sprinkle with the spices, mixed together, and the grated rind of half the lemon. Repeat the layers, and put a final layer of breadcrumbs on top, dotted with margarine. Mix the juice of the lemon with a teacupful of water and pour over the pudding. Bake for 45 minutes in a moderate oven.
Cooking Time: 1 hour/6-8 Helpings

Coconut Orange Pudding

225g/8oz self-raising flour
75g/3oz margarine
75g/3 tablespoonfuls golden syrup
50g/2oz desiccated coconut
300ml/½ pint milk
I orange

Rub the margarine into the flour, add the coconut and the grated rind of the orange. Mix the golden syrup with the milk and pour it on the mixture. Prepare a pudding basin or pie dish by brushing it with melted margarine. Put in the pudding mixture, steam for 2 hours, covered with a doubled paper brushed with margarine, or bake for 50 minutes in a moderately hot oven. Serve with the juice of an orange mixed with golden syrup.

Cooking Time: 2 hours/6-8 Helpings

Prices of
DRIED FRUITS

From tomorrow dried fruits
will be classified into 3 groups
with a maximum price for each
group, so that you will be able
to buy what there is at really
reasonable prices throughout the
United Kingdom.

Dates — 7d. per lb.

Currants
Muscatels
Raisins
Sultanas
Dried Apples
Dried Plums and
Prunes other
than Prunes
canned in syrup
Figs
} 9d. per lb.

Dried Apricots
Dried Nectarines
Dried Peaches
Dried Pears
} 1/- per lb.

★ FAIR SHARES OF DRIED FRUITS!
SEE IMPORTANT MINISTRY OF FOOD
ANNOUNCEMENT IN THIS ISSUE

Coconut Orange Pudding

Florida Pudding

450g/1lb stale cake or, better still, gingerbread
1 tin of peaches
25g/1oz desiccated coconut
25g/1oz margarine

Cut the stale cake in square pieces. Put a layer of
cake into a pie dish and pour some of the syrup
from the peaches over it. Slice the peaches and
lay them on top of the cake adding the rest of
the syrup. Leave to soak for half an hour, then
dot with margarine and sprinkle with coconut.
Bake for 1 hour in a moderate oven.
Cooking Time: 2 hours/6 Helpings

Orange Mould

50g/2oz cornflour
600ml/1 pint milk
25g/1oz sugar
Rind and juice of $1/2$ orange
$1/2$ orange for decoration
12g/$1/2$oz margarine

Patsy

Learn To Cook By Pictures
2/6

MILITARY SECRETS
MUST BE GUARDED
IN PEACE AND WAR

DO NOT
DISCUSS THEM
IN PUBLIC

Blend the cornflour with a little cold milk, put
the rest of the milk on to boil. When the milk
comes to the boil, pour it on to the blended
cornflour, stirring well. Add the grated rind of
the orange, cut the orange in half and add the
juice from one half. Add this also to the cornflour. Return the mixture to the saucepan, add
the margarine and boil; boil for five minutes,
stirring all the time. Add the sugar and pour into
the jelly mould. When cold and set, turn onto a
glass dish and decorate with pieces of orange.
Cooking Time: 30 minutes/2 Helpings

Baked Sultana Cake Pudding

225g/8oz pieces of cake
50ml/2oz sultanas
300ml/¹/2 pint milk
1 egg
Sugar to taste

Place a layer of cake in the bottom of a pie dish, brushed with melted margarine, sprinkle with a few sultanas and a little sugar, and repeat these layers until the ingredients are used up. Mix the beaten egg with the milk and pour over the dry ingredients. Bake in a fairly hot oven for 50 minutes. Serve with custard.
Cooking Time: 1 hour/4 Helpings

Lemon Tart

150g/6oz short crust or biscuit crust
3 tablespoonfuls lemon curd (see below)

Make the pastry and roll to a round. Brush a pie plate with melted margarine, fit the round of pastry into it. Spread the lemon curd over it, trim the edges. Roll out the trimmings, cut thin strips from them and decorate the top of the tart. Bake 25-30 minutes in a moderately hot oven.
Cooking Time: 1 hour/4-6 Helpings

EVERY CRUMB COUNTS

Never throw away stale bread. Use it as breadcrumbs in a breakfast cereal, or crush them for coatings. Soak, squeeze and beat up with a fork for sweet and savoury puddings, etc.

Wartime Lemon Curd

25g/1oz margarine
1 level tablespoonful cornflour
2 lemons
150ml/¼ pint water
125g/5oz granulated sugar
1 egg

Peel the rind off the lemons very thinly (a potato peeler is the best thing to use for this purpose). Put the rind into the 150ml/¼ pint of water and bring to the boil. Beat the egg and blend the cornflour with it, taking care to make the mixture smooth; mixing egg and cornflour makes it possible to boil the mixture without curdling the egg. Add the lemon juice and strain the boiling water over the mixture, stirring well. Return to the pan, add the sugar and stir over the heat for 3 minutes. Add the margarine, stir it well in and pour into a basin to cool.
Cooking Time: 30 minutes/10 Helpings